THI

E

F

CHAT-UP
LINES

Jake Harris

summersdale

THE LITTLE BOOK OF ESSENTIAL FOREIGN CHAT-UP LINES

Summersdale Publishers Ltd
46 West Street
Chichester
West Sussex
PO19 1RP
UK

www.summersdale.com

Printed and bound in Great Britain

ISBN: 1-84024-579-4
ISBN 13: 978-1-84024-579-0

With thanks to Giovanni and Antonella Montagano, Nils Feldmann, Luis Zapardiel, Anne-Sophie Perrin and Benedicte Jorrot for their help with translations.

Introduction

Let's face facts. Foreigners are hot. They're exotic, they're cultured, and they like to have sex outdoors. And when you're abroad, the natives think you're hot too, so what better way to embrace this fact than by testing out your chatting-up skills?

Language barriers mean less 'chin-wag' and more 'great shag', but how do you get the guy or girl to notice you in the first place? Unless you're the sexiest thing this side of the Med, chances are your moves on the dance floor and 'interesting' holiday fashion ain't gonna cut it. A witty opening line and dazzling smile ought to do the trick for a night of fun.

So brush up on your accents and make the most of these classic come-ons. And for the dogs that try and dig their claws into you – I've included some foreign-friendly put-downs to get you out of those sticky situations.

Just remember – saying anything SLOWLY and LOUDLY in ENGLEEESH is more likely to earn you a slap in the face than on the arse. So be bold and brave and woo those sexy locals with your well-travelled tongue. And you never know... your tongue might end up having a really good time!

THE LITTLE BOOK OF

"
Hi, I'm Mr Right. I heard you were looking for me.
"

ITALIAN:

Salve, sono il l'uomo Giusto. Mi stava forse
cercando?

GERMAN:

Hallo, ich bin der Traummann. Du hast nach
mir gesucht?

FRENCH:

Bonjour, je suis l'homme idéal! Tu me
cherchais?

SPANISH:

Hola, soy don Perfecto. Me han dicho que
andabas buscándome.

" Is it hot in here or is it just you? "

ITALIAN:

Fa sempre caldo qui o è la sua presenza?

GERMAN:

Ist es heiss hier drinnen, oder bist du das?

FRENCH:

Tu n'trouves pas qu´il fait chaud ici? Ou est-ce toi qui me fais cet effet?

SPANISH:

¿Hace calor o eres tú?

"

I think we should leave together for the sake of the other women here... you're making them look ugly.

"

ITALIAN:

Penso che dovremmo andarcene insieme per il bene delle altre donne qui presenti… le fa apparire tutte brutte.

GERMAN:

Ich denke wir sollten gehen, der anderen Frauen wegen ... neben dir sehen sie alle hässlich aus.

FRENCH:

Il vaudrait mieux que l'on s'en aille tout de suite ensemble… Pense aux autres femmes ici… Elles paraissent si laides à côté de toi!

SPANISH:

Creo que deberíamos irnos por el bien de las otras mujeres… las estás haciendo parecer muy feas.

" Do you think if I'm really good this year, Father Christmas will put you in my stocking? "

ITALIAN:

Se quest'anno sarò davvero buono, pensi che Babbo Natale mi porterà in dono anche te?

GERMAN:

Wenn ich in diesem Jahr ganz brav bin, legt dich der Weihnachtsmann dann unter meinen Baum?

FRENCH:

Tu crois que si je suis très gentil cette année, le Père Noël te mettra dans mes cadeaux?

SPANISH:

¿Crees que si me porto muy bien este año Papá Noel te pondrá en mi calcetín?

" Excuse me, I seem to have lost my phone number, can I borrow yours? "

ITALIAN:

Mi scusi, credo di aver perso il mio numero di telefono, potrebbe prestarmi il suo?

GERMAN:

Tschuldigung, ich habe meine Telefonnummer verloren. Kann ich Deine haben?

FRENCH:

Excuse-moi, j´ai oublié mon numéro de téléphone. Je peux emprunter le tien?

SPANISH:

Perdona, me parece que he perdido mi número de teléfono, ¿me prestas el tuyo?

It's my birthday, how about a birthday kiss?

ITALIAN:

E' il mio compleanno, perché non mi dai un bacio per farmi gli auguri?

GERMAN:

Ich habe heute Geburtstag, wie wär's mit einem Geburtstagskuss?

FRENCH:

C´est mon anniversaire aujourd´hui. Et si on s´embrassait?

SPANISH:

Es mi cumple, ¿qué tal un besito de cumpleaños?

THE LITTLE BOOK OF

"

Let me introduce myself: I'm your future husband.

"

ITALIAN:

Lasci che mi presenti: Sono il suo futuro marito.

GERMAN:

Darf ich mich vorstellen: ich bin dein künftiger Ehemann.

FRENCH:

Permets-moi de me présenter: c'est moi! Ton futur mari!

SPANISH:

Permíteme que me presente: Soy tu futuro marido.

" You're so hot you'd make the devil sweat!

ITALIAN:

Sei così calda che riusciresti a
sciogliere persino il diavolo.

GERMAN:

Du bist so scharf, da fängt sogar
der Teufel an zu schwitzen.

FRENCH:

Tu es tellement craquante que
le diable en transpirerait!

SPANISH:

Eres tan caliente que podrías hacer sudar al
mismísmo diablo.

" **When God made you, he was showing off.** "

ITALIAN:
Creandoti, Dio volle mettersi in mostra.

GERMAN:
Als Gott dich geschaffen hat, wollte er angeben.

FRENCH:
Quand Dieu t'a créée, il s'est surpassé!

SPANISH:
Cuando Dios te creó, se lució.

All those curves, and me with no brakes...

ITALIAN:

Con tutte quelle curve avrei bisogno di freni…

GERMAN:

All diese Kurven, und ich ohne Bremsen ...

FRENCH:

Toutes ces formes me font
perdre mes moyens…

SPANISH:

Todas esas curves, y yo sin frenos…

> **" I would buy you a drink but I would be jealous of the glass. "**

ITALIAN:

Vorrei offrirle da bere, ma sarei geloso del bicchiere.

GERMAN:

Ich könnte dir ja einen ausgeben, aber dann ware ich neidisch auf das Glas.

FRENCH:

Je t'offrirais bien un verre, mais je pourrais en être jaloux…

SPANISH:

Te invitaría a tomar algo, pero me pondría celoso del vaso.

"

There must be something wrong with my eyes; I can't take them off you.

"

ITALIAN:

Devo avere qualche problema con miei occhi; non riesco a toglierglieli di dosso.

GERMAN:

Irgendwas stimmt mit meinen Augen nicht: die bleiben immer an dir hängen.

FRENCH:

Je dois avoir un problème aux yeux; je ne peux pas m´empêcher de te regarder…

SPANISH:

Debo de tener un problema con la vista; no la puedo apartar de ti.

" I like to think it's my vocation to make women happy in bed. "

ITALIAN:

Mi piace pensare che fare felici le
donne a letto è la mia missione.

GERMAN:

Ich glaube es ist meine Berufung,
Frauen im Bett glücklich zu machen.

FRENCH:

Je suis né pour rendre les
femmes heureuses au lit.

SPANISH:

Me gusta pensar que es mi vocación
hacer feliz a las mujeres en la cama.

If you kiss me, I promise I won't turn into a frog.

ITALIAN:

Te lo prometto, se mi baci non mi trasformerò
in un rospo.

GERMAN:

Wenn du mich küsst verspreche ich, nicht
zum Frosch zu werden.

FRENCH:

Si tu m'embrasses, je te promets de ne pas
me transformer en crapaud.

SPANISH:

Si me besas, te prometo no convertirme
en rana.

"

You know what I like best about you? All of you.

"

ITALIAN:

Sai qual è la cosa che mi piace di più di te?
Tutto.

GERMAN:

Was mir an dir am besten gefällt? Alles.

FRENCH:

Sais-tu ce que j'aime le plus en toi? Tout!

SPANISH:

¿Sabes lo que más me gusta de ti? Toda tú.

"You're so hot you melt the elastic in my underwear."

ITALIAN:

Sei così calda che hai sciolto l'elastico della mio slip.

GERMAN:

Du bist so heiss, da schmilzt das Gummiband in meiner Unterhose.

FRENCH:

Tu es tellement chaude que tu fais fondre l'élastique de mon caleçon!

SPANISH:

Eres tan caliente que has derretido el elástico de mis calzoncillos.

That dress would look great in a crumpled heap on my bedroom floor.

ITALIAN:

Quel vestito starebbe benissimo sgualcito sul pavimento della mia camera da letto.

GERMAN:

Das Kleid könnte ich mir auch ganz gut zerknautscht auf meinem Schlafzimmer-Fussboden vorstellen.

FRENCH:

Cette robe serait grandiose jetée sur le sol de ma chambre...

SPANISH:

Ese vestido quedaría genial arrugado y tirado en el suelo de mi dormitorio.

"You're the kind of girl I'd like to take home to mother except I wouldn't trust my father."

ITALIAN:

Sei il tipo di ragazza che presenterei
volentieri a mia madre ma non a mio padre.

GERMAN:

Ich würde dich ja gern meiner Mutter
vorstellen, aber ich traue meinem Vater nicht.

FRENCH:

Tu es le genre de femme que je présenterais
bien à ma mère, mais pas à mon père!

SPANISH:

Eres la clase de chica que me gustaría llevar
a casa de mi madre, salvo que no me fiaría
de mi padre.

"

You're so beautiful; I've forgotten my chat-up line.

"

ITALIAN:

Sei una bellezza mozzafiato! Ho dimenticato la battuta che mi ero preparato.

GERMAN:

Du bist so traumhaft schön, da habe ich glatt meine Anmache vergessen.

FRENCH:

Tu es tellement belle que j'en oublie ma méthode de drague!

SPANISH:

Eres tan guapa; he olvidad cómo te iba a entrar.

"God ordered me to come to you."

ITALIAN:

È Dio che mi manda da te.

GERMAN:

Gott hat mir befohlen dich anzusprechen.

FRENCH:

Dieu m'a ordonné de venir à toi.

SPANISH:

Dios me ha enviado a estar contigo.

"

What's it like being the most attractive person for miles around?

"

ITALIAN:
Cosa si prova ad essere la persona più attraente nel raggio di chilometri e chilometri?

GERMAN:
Und wie ist es so, wenn man die attraktivste Person weit und breit ist?

FRENCH:
Quel effet ça fait d'être la plus belle à des kilomètres à la ronde?

SPANISH:
¿Cómo se siente al ser la persona más atractiva en kilómetros a la redodanda?

"

You and me would look sweet together on a wedding cake.

"

ITALIAN:

Che carini che saremmo io e te su una torta nuziale.

GERMAN:

Du und ich: das würde sich gut machen auf der Hochzeitstorte.

FRENCH:

On serait mignons tous les deux en miniatures en haut d'une pièce montée…

SPANISH:

Tú y yo quedaríamos de rechupete en un pastel de boda.

THE LITTLE BOOK OF

" **Excuse me, I want to be served by the most attractive waitress. You do work here, don't you?** "

ITALIAN:

Scusami, voglio che a servirmi sia la cameriera più attraente che c'è. Tu lavori qui, giusto?

GERMAN:

Entschuldigung, ich würde gerne von der schönsten Kellnerin bedient werden. Du arbeitest doch hier, oder?

FRENCH:

Excuse-moi, j'aimerais etre servi par l'employée la plus sexy. Tu travailles ici n'est-ce pas?

SPANISH:

Perdona, me gustaría que me atendiera la camarera más atractiva. Tú trabajas aquí, ¿no?

THE LITTLE BOOK OF

" **It must be my birthday because the sight of you is the best gift I've ever had.** "

ITALIAN:

Dovrebbe essere oggi il mio compleanno perché la visione di te è il più bel regalo che io abbia mai avuto.

GERMAN:

Es muss wohl mein Geburtstag sein – und dich zu treffen das schönste Geschenk.

FRENCH:

Ce doit être mon anniversaire, parce que le fait de te voir est le plus beau cadeau que j'ai jamais eu!

SPANISH:

Debe de ser mi cumpleaños porque verte es el mejor regalo que jamás he tenido.

" If I could see you naked, I'd die happy. "

ITALIAN:

Se potessi vederti nuda, morirei felice.

GERMAN:

Wenn ich dich nackt sehen könnte,
würde ich glücklich sterben.

FRENCH:

Si je pouvais te voir entièrement
nue, je mourrais heureux.

SPANISH:

Si pudiera verte desnuda, moriría feliz.

Apart from being sexy, what else do you do?

ITALIAN:

Oltre ad essere così sexy,
di cos'altro ti occupi?

GERMAN:

Was machst du denn sonst so,
ausser geil auszusehen.

FRENCH:

À part être sexy, tu fais quoi dans la vie?

SPANISH:

Además de ser tan sexy, ¿qué
más sabes hacer?

If you were a laser gun, you'd be set on stunning.

ITALIAN:

Se tu fossi una pistola laser,
saresti usata per accecare.

GERMAN:

Wenn du 'ne Laserwaffe wärst,
wärst du auf Umhauen gestellt.

FRENCH:

Si tu étais une arme, tu serais dévastatrice.

SPANISH:

Si fueras una pistola láser,
aturdirías al disparar.

"

This isn't a beer belly; it's a fuel tank for a love machine.

"

ITALIAN:
Questa non è una pancia da birra, È piuttosto una riserva di benzina per una macchina del sesso.

GERMAN:
Das ist keine Wampe, sondern der Tank meiner Wundermaschine.

FRENCH:
Ce ne sont pas des poignées d'amour, mais des kilos de tendresse à donner!

SPANISH:
Esto no es una barriga cervecera; es un tanque de combustible para una máquina de amar.

"

Go on, don't be shy: ask me out.

"

ITALIAN:

Dai, continua, non essere timido:
chiedimi un appuntamento!

GERMAN:

Na los, trau' dich: Lad' mich zum Essen ein.

FRENCH:

Allez, ne sois pas timide, demande-
moi de sortir avec toi!

SPANISH:

Venga, no seas tímida: pídeme salir.

"

I'm afraid I'll have to call the police, because it's got to be illegal to look as good as you.

"

ITALIAN:

Temo che sarò costretto a chiamare la polizia, perché avere un così bel aspetto come il suo deve essere illegale.

GERMAN:

Ich muss leider die Polizei rufen, denn es ist verboten, so gut auszusehen wie du.

FRENCH:

J'ai peur de devoir appeler la police… C'est sûrement illégal d'être aussi belle!

SPANISH:

Lo siento pero tendré que llamar a la policía, seguro que es ilegal estar tan buena.

My horoscope said I would meet the woman of my dreams tonight.

ITALIAN:

Il mio oroscopo diceva che stanotte avrei conosciuto la donna dei miei sogni.

GERMAN:

Mein Horoskop sagt mir, dass ich heute die Frau meiner Träume treffe.

FRENCH:

Mon horoscope m'a prédit que je rencontrerai la femme de ma vie ce soir.

SPANISH:

Mi horóscopo dice que conoceré a la mujer de mis sueños esta noche.

"

Don't go – we may never find each other again.

"

ITALIAN:

Non andare via, potremmo non incontrarci
mai più.

GERMAN:

Geh' nicht – wir könnten uns aus den Augen
verlieren.

FRENCH:

Ne t'en va pas, on pourrait ne jamais se
revoir.

SPANISH:

No te vayas – puede que no volvamos a
encontrarnos otra vez.

"

You've got a smile that could light up a whole town.

"

ITALIAN:

Il tuo sorriso potrebbe illuminare una città intera.

GERMAN:

Dein Lächeln könnte die ganze Stadt zum Leuchten bringen.

FRENCH:

Ton sourire pourrait illuminer une ville entière.

SPANISH:

Tienes una sonrisa que podría iluminar una ciudad entera.

"Which side of my bed would you like to sleep on?"

ITALIAN:
Su quale lato del mio letto ti piacerebbe dormire?

GERMAN:
Auf welcher Seite vom Bett möchtest du schlafen?

FRENCH:
Quel côté du lit est-ce que tu préfères?

SPANISH:
¿En qué lado de mi cama prefieres dormir?

What can I do to get a little kiss from you?

ITALIAN:

Cosa devo fare per avere un tuo bacio?

GERMAN:

Und was kann ich tun, um ein Küsschen zu bekommen?

FRENCH:

Que dois-je faire pour avoir un petit baiser?

SPANISH:

¿Que puedo hacer para que me des un beso?

"

I may be a bit of an eyesore, but beauty is only a light switch away.

"

ITALIAN:

Potrei anche essere un po' un pugno in un occhio, ma la bellezza non è nient'altro che un leggero passaggio.

GERMAN:

Ich bin vielleicht hässlich, aber wir können ja einfach das Licht ausmachen.

FRENCH:

Je n'ai peut-être pas un physique avantageux, mais il suffit d'éteindre la lumière…

SPANISH:

Puedo parecer un poco feo, pero la belleza está tan solo a un interruptor de distancia.

The more I drink, the prettier you get.

ITALIAN:

Più bevo più mi sembri bella.

GERMAN:

Je mehr ich trinke, desto hübscher wirst du.

FRENCH:

Plus je bois, plus tu es belle.

SPANISH:

Cuanto más bebo, más guapa te pones.

"Hey, don't go yet... you've forgotten something. Me!"

ITALIAN:

Hey, non andare via subito… hai dimenticato qualcosa. Me!

GERMAN:

Du kannst noch nicht gehen … du hast 'was vergessen. Mich!

FRENCH:

Ne pars pas déjà! Tu oublies quelque chose: moi!

SPANISH:

Eh, no te vayas todavía… te dejas algo. ¡A mí!

I'm learning to be an artist and I'd like to paint you.

ITALIAN:

Sto per diventare un artista e mi piacerebbe dipingerti.

GERMAN:

Ich studiere Malerei und würde dich gerne malen.

FRENCH:

Je suis étudiant en peinture, et tu ferais un modèle parfait!

SPANISH:

Estoy aprendiendo a ser un artista y me encantaría pintarte.

"

What winks and is great in bed? (Wink).

"

ITALIAN:

Come ammicca bene! Lo sa fare anche a letto? (Ammiccamento).

GERMAN:

Was zwinkert und ist gut im Bett? (Zwinker).

FRENCH:

Qu'est-ce qui fait des clins d'œil et assure au pieu? (Clin d'œil).

SPANISH:

¿Quién hace un guiño y es genial en la cama? (Guiña un ojo).

66

I bet you can't give me three good reasons why I shouldn't buy you a drink.

99

ITALIAN:

Scommetto che non sapresti darmi tre buoni motivi per cui non dovrei pagarti da bere!

GERMAN:

Kannst du mir drei Gründe nennen, warum ich dir keinen ausgeben sollte? Ich wette nicht.

FRENCH:

Je te parie que tu ne me donnes pas trois bonnes raisons de ne pas t'offrir un verre!

SPANISH:

Me apuesto algo a que no puedes darme tres buenas rezones para que no te invite a tomar algo.

"

Hey gorgeous! That is your name, right?

"

ITALIAN:
Hei bellissima! E' questo il suo nome, vero?

GERMAN:
Hallo Schönheit. So heist du doch, oder?

FRENCH:
Salut Beauté! C'est bien ton nom n'est-ce pas?

SPANISH:
¡Hola preciosidad! Ese es tu nombre, ¿no?

THE LITTLE BOOK OF

"

If you think you might regret this in the morning, we can stay in bed until the afternoon.

"

ITALIAN:

Se pensi che in mattinata potresti rimpiangere quello che hai fatto, perché non restiamo a letto fino al pomeriggio?

GERMAN:

Falls du Angst hast, es könnte dir am nächsten Morgen leid tut, können wir ja einfach bis nachmittags im Bett bleiben.

FRENCH:

Si tu as peur de le regretter au petit matin, on peut rester au lit jusque dans l'après-midi!

SPANISH:

Si piensas que lo lamentarás por la mañana, nos podemos quedar en la cama hasta el mediodía.

" If I had a penny for every time I saw a girl as stunning as you I'd end up completely broke. "

ITALIAN:

Se mi dessero un centesimo per ogni volta che ho visto ragazze del tuo stesso splendore ora sarei completamente al verde.

GERMAN:

Wenn ich jedes Mal einen Cent bekommen würde, wenn ich eine so schöne Frau sehe, ware ich total pleite.

FRENCH:

Si je gagnais un centime chaque fois que je vois une femme aussi belle que toi, je serais complètement fauché!

SPANISH:

Si consiguiera un euro por cada vez que viera a una chica tan guapa como tú, no tendría un duro.

I bet you twenty quid you're going to turn me down.

ITALIAN:

Scommetto venti euros che stai per darmi un due di picche.

GERMAN:

Ich wette mit dir um zwanzig euros, dass du mich abblitzen lässt.

FRENCH:

Je te parie vingt euros que tu vas me laisser tomber.

SPANISH:

Te apuesto veinte euros a que me vas a decir que no.

Do you believe in love at first sight or should I walk past you again?

ITALIAN:

Credi nell'amore a prima vista oppure devo ripassarti davanti?

GERMAN:

Glaubst du an Liebe auf den ersten Blick, oder soll ich gleich nochmal vorbeikommen?

FRENCH:

Crois-tu au coup de foudre, ou devrais-je insister?

SPANISH:

¿Crees en el amor a primera vista o prefieres que pase por delante tuya otra vez?

" You're just like a girlfriend of mine. My next one. "

ITALIAN:

Somigli proprio ad una delle mie ragazze. La prossima.

GERMAN:

Du hast was von 'ner Freundin von mir. Von meiner nächsten Freundin.

FRENCH:

Tu ressembles beaucoup à une de mes anciennes petites amies. D'ailleurs c'est bien simple, tu es la prochaine…

SPANISH:

Eres como una de mis novias. La próxima.

THE LITTLE BOOK OF

"

Your eyes are like spanners; every time I see you my nuts tighten.

"

ITALIAN:

I tuoi occhi sono come chiavi inglesi; Ogni volta che ti vedo i miei testicoli si stringono.

GERMAN:

Hast du vielleicht 'ne Eieruhr dabei? Wenn du mich noch lange so anguckst, sind meine gleich hart.

FRENCH:

Tes yeux ont un pouvoir télescopique; chaque fois que je croise ton regard, mon tuyau s'allonge...

SPANISH:

Tus ojos son como llaves; cada vez que te veo se me aprietan las tuercas.

THE LITTLE BOOK OF

"

How about you sit on my lap and we straighten things out?

"

ITALIAN:

Perché non ti siedi sulle mie gambe e sistemiamo le cose?

GERMAN:

Also, du setzt dich auf meinen Schoss und wir unterhalten uns drüber.

FRENCH:

Et si tu venais sur mes genoux et qu'on tirait les choses au clair tous les deux?

SPANISH:

¿Por qué no te sientas en mis rodillas y aclaramos un par de cosas?

You're like a four leaf clover: hard to find and lucky to have.

ITALIAN:
Sei come un trifoglio con quattro foglie: è difficile trovarlo, ma chi lo trova è fortunato.

GERMAN:
Du bist wie ein vierblättriges Kleeblatt: Eines zu finden ist ein grosses Glück.

FRENCH:
Tu es comme un trèfle à quatre feuilles: rare et précieuse…

SPANISH:
Eres como un trébol de cuatro hojas: difícil de encontrar y trae suerte.

" Well, here I am. What are your other two wishes? "

ITALIAN:

Lo sono qui, eccomi. Quali sono i tuoi due altri desideri?

GERMAN:

Also hier bin ich. Und was waren deine anderen beiden Wünsche?

FRENCH:

Voilà, je suis là! Quels sont tes deux autres voeux?

SPANISH:

Bueno ya estoy aquí. ¿Cuáles son tus otros deseos?

"

Can I take your photo please, so I can show Santa what I'd like for Christmas?

"

ITALIAN:

Potrei farle una foto? Vorrei mostrare a Babbo Natale cosa voglio per Natale.

GERMAN:

Ich brauche dein Foto, damit der Weihnachtsmann weiss, was ich mir wünsche.

FRENCH:

Je peux te prendre en photo pour montrer au Père Noël ce que je veux cette année?

SPANISH:

¿Me puedes dar una foto tuya para enseñarle a Papá Noel qué quiero para Navidad?

"

I need a place to blot my lipstick... can I use your lips?

"

ITALIAN:

Ho bisogno di un posto per togliermi il rossetto… posso usare le tue labbra?

GERMAN:

Ich muss mal eben irgendwo meinen Lippenstift abwischen ... wie wär's mit deinem Mund?

FRENCH:

Il faut que j'estompe mon gloss… Ça t'embête si j'emprunte tes lèvres?

SPANISH:

Necesito algo para quitarme el carmín… ¿puedo usar tus labios?

"

Hello there, do you know the weight of a polar bear? Neither do I, but it breaks the ice!

"

ITALIAN:

Salve, per caso lei sa quanto pesa un orso polare? Neppure io, ma serve a rompere il ghiaccio!

GERMAN:

Weisst du wie schwer ein Eisbär ist? Ich auch nicht, aber bei der Frage tauen eigentlich alle Frauen auf!

FRENCH:

Salut! Tu sais combien pèse un ours polaire? … Moi non plus, mais au moins ça brise la glace!

SPANISH:

Hola, ¿sabes cuánto pesa un oso polar? Yo tampoco, pero ¡rompe el hielo!

" **You're so hot. It's girls like you that cause global warming.** "

ITALIAN:

Sei così focosa. Sono le ragazze come te
a causare il surriscaldamento della terra.

GERMAN:

Du bist so heiss, kein Wunder
dass das Polareis schmilzt.

FRENCH:

Tu es si sexy... Ce sont les filles comme toi
qui entraînent le réchauffement de la planète!

SPANISH:

Eres tan caliente. Chicas como tú sois
la causa del recalentamiento global.

I'm afraid I can't go out/go on a date with you because...

ITALIAN:

Mi dispiace ma non posso uscire con te perché…

GERMAN:

Ich befürchte ich kann mich
nicht mit dir treffen, weil...

FRENCH:

Je suis désolée, mais je ne peux
pas sortir avec toi parce que…

SPANISH:

Lo siento no puedo salir contigo porque…

THE LITTLE BOOK OF

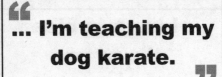

... I'm teaching my dog karate.

ITALIAN:
... insegno karate al mio cane.

GERMAN:
... ich meinem Hund gerade Karate beibringe.

FRENCH:
... c'est l'heure du cours de karaté de mon chien.

SPANISH:
... estoy enseñando karate a mi perro.

" ... I have to clean the oven. "

ITALIAN:
... devo pulire il forno.

GERMAN:
... ich den Backofen sauber machen muss.

FRENCH:
... je dois nettoyer mon four.

SPANISH:
... tengo que limpiar el horno.

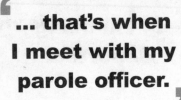

... that's when I meet with my parole officer.

ITALIAN:
... ho appuntamento con il mio portavoce.

GERMAN:
...ich einen Termin bei meinem Bewehrungshelfer habe.

FRENCH:
... j'ai rendez-vous avec mon ex-gardien de prison.

SPANISH:
... tengo que ver al oficial de la condicional.

" ... I'm being deported. "

ITALIAN:
... sono in esilio.

GERMAN:
... ich gerade abgeschoben werde.

FRENCH:
... je dois être expulsée du pays.

SPANISH:
... me van a deportar.

" I'd love to come out with you... "

ITALIAN:

Mi piacerebbe tanto uscire con te…

GERMAN:

Ich würde mich gerne mit dir treffen…

FRENCH:

J'adorerais sortir avec toi…

SPANISH:

Me encantaría salir contigo…

" ... but the voices in my head say no. "

ITALIAN:

... ma le voci che sento nella mia testa mi dicono di non farlo.

GERMAN:

... mein zweites Ich sagt Nein.

FRENCH:

... mais les voix dans ma tête me disent de ne pas le faire.

SPANISH:

... pero las voces en mi cabeza dicen no.

" ... as long as I can bring my mother. "

ITALIAN:

... ma solo a condizione che venga anche mia madre.

GERMAN:

... nur wenn meine Mutter mitkommt.

FRENCH:

... mais seulement si ma mère vient avec nous.

SPANISH:

... siempre y cuando pueda traer a mi madre.

" ... I'm homeless, so where do you want to pick me up from? "

ITALIAN:
... sono un barbone, dove preferisci venire a prendermi?

GERMAN:
... ich bin obdachlos. Wo willst du mich denn abholen?

FRENCH:
... au fait, je suis SDF. Ou passes-tu me prendre?

SPANISH:
... soy un sin techo, así que ¿dónde me recoges?

Celebrity Chat-Up Lines

Stewart Ferris

£2.99

ISBN: 978 1 84024 540 0

Just because they're rich, beautiful and successful doesn't mean that famous people don't have trouble pulling. This hilarious collection contains all the chat-up lines celebrities wish they could think of to have babes and blokes falling at their feet.

'You've heard of Henman Hill: now it's called Murray Mount. Let me show you how it works.'

A suggested chat-up line for Andy Murray

'Shut up and get in my f!#ing bed now, you #*!^%$ @{}*<>&$*!'*

A suggested chat-up line for Kelly Osbourne

www.summersdale.com